1/27/10

Louisburg Library District No. 1

206 S. Broadway St.

Louisburg, KS 66053

913-837-2217

www.louisburglibrary.org

DEMCO

FAVORITE BASKETBALL TEAMS

New York Knicks

Louisburg Library
Bringing People and Information Together

BY K. C. KELLEY

THE CHILD'S WORLD®
1980 Lookout Drive • Mankato, MN 56003-1705
800-599-READ • www.childsworld.com

ACKNOWLEDGMENTS

The Child's World®: Mary Berendes, Publishing Director
Shoreline Publishing Group, LLC: James Buckley, Jr., Production Director
The Design Lab: Kathleen Petelinsek, Design; Gregory Lindholm, Page Production

PHOTOS

Cover and interior: AP/Wide World Photos

Published in the United States of America.

LIBRARY OF CONGRESS
CATALOGING-IN-PUBLICATION DATA

Kelley, K. C.
  New York Knicks / by K.C. Kelley.
      p. cm. — (Favorite basketball teams)
  Includes bibliographical references and index.
  ISBN 978-1-60253-311-0 (library bound : alk. paper)
  1. New York Knickerbockers (Basketball team)—Juvenile literature.
  2. Basketball—New York (State)—New York—Juvenile literature.
  I. Title. II. Series.
  GV885.52.N4K45 2009
  796.323'64097471—dc22   2009009792

Table of Contents

Go, Knicks!

New York City is one of the biggest cities in the world. Its top basketball team is the New York Knicks. The Knicks' name is actually short for Knickerbockers. That's what some of the first people from Europe to live in New York were called. The Knicks are one of the oldest and most popular teams in the NBA. Let's head to New York City and meet the Knicks!

David Lee is one of the Knicks' best all-around stars.

Nate Robinson and a teammate celebrate a big win.

Who Are the Knicks?

The New York Knicks play in the National Basketball Association (NBA). They are one of 30 teams in the NBA. The NBA includes the Eastern Conference and the Western Conference. The Knicks play in the Atlantic Division of the Eastern Conference. The winner of the Eastern Conference plays the winner of the Western Conference in the **NBA Finals**. The Knicks have been the NBA champions twice.

Where They Came From

The New York Knicks were one of the first teams in the NBA. They started playing in 1946, in a league called the Basketball Association of America (BAA). In 1949, the BAA joined with another league to become the NBA. The Knicks got off to a hot start in the NBA. They made the **playoffs** nine times in their first 10 years. They won their first NBA championship in 1970.

9

Willis Reed (19) led the Knicks to their first title in 1970.

The Knicks and the Nets are neighbors . . . and rivals.

Who They Play

The Knicks play 82 games each season. That's a lot of basketball! They play every other NBA team at least once each season. They play teams in their division and conference more often. Since the 1950s, the Knicks have had a big **rivalry** with the Boston Celtics. Knicks fans also look forward to games with the New Jersey Nets. New Jersey is right next to New York.

Where They Play

The Knicks play their home games at Madison Square Garden. It is one of the most famous basketball arenas in the world. Many important games and **tournaments** have been played there. It is also the scene of rock concerts, big meetings, and circuses. Today's Madison Square Garden opened in 1968. Three other buildings called Madison Square Garden were the Knicks' home before then.

Madison Square Garden is the home of some great basketball action.

13

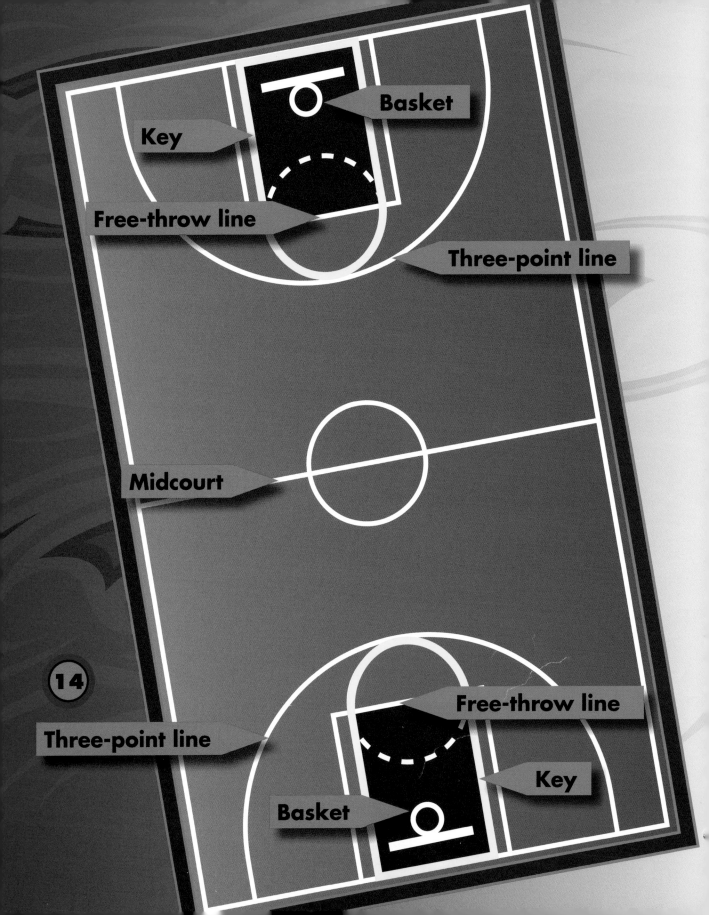

Basket

Key

Free-throw line

Three-point line

Midcourt

Free-throw line

Three-point line

Key

Basket

The Basketball Court

Basketball is played on a court made of wood. An NBA court is 94 feet (29 m) long. A painted line shows the middle of the court. Other lines lay out the free-throw area. The space below each basket is known as the "key." The baskets at each end are 10 feet (3 m) off the ground. The metal rims of the baskets stick out over the court. Nylon nets hang from the rims.

Big Days!

The New York Knicks have had many great moments in their long history. Here are three of the greatest:

1970: Center **Willis Reed was injured before the last game of the NBA Finals. He limped onto the court to play for just a few moments. His courage inspired his teammates. They won the championship!**

1973: **The Knicks won their second NBA championship.**

1994: **The Knicks finished with one of the best records in the NBA. However, they lost the Finals to the Houston Rockets.**

Reed was healthy when the Knicks won again in 1973.

In this 2002 game against Boston, nothing went right for the Knicks.

Tough Days!

The Knicks can't win all their games. Some games or seasons don't turn out well. The players keep trying to play their best, though! Here are some of the toughest seasons in Knicks history:

1961: The Knicks won only 21 games—their lowest number ever!

2002: The Knicks lost to their rivals, the Boston Celtics, 104–59. They lost this game by more points than any other game in their history!

2009: The Knicks missed the playoffs for the fifth straight year.

Meet the Fans

Knicks fans love basketball. They are also very loud! They fill Madison Square Garden and go crazy to support their team. When the team is doing well, they let the players know it. But when the Knicks aren't doing well, the fans don't mind booing! The team has had a few slow years, but the fans still love their Knicks.

Fans sitting close to the court sometimes get players in their laps!

Walt Frazier shows off his great dribbling skills.

Heroes Then...

The Knicks won two championships thanks to several great players. **Guard** Walt Frazier was a great dribbler and passer. Guard Earl "The Pearl" Monroe could also dribble—and shoot—very well. At center, Willis Reed played great **defense** and grabbed lots of **rebounds**. **Forward** Bill Bradley was a star on **offense**. He could hit shots from many parts of the court. (He later became a U.S. Senator from New Jersey!) In the 1980s and 1990s, center Patrick Ewing led the Knicks. He was one of the best "big men" in the NBA.

Heroes Now...

In 2008, Al Harrington left the Golden State Warriors and joined the Knicks. He brought a great shooting touch and speed to the team. Forward David Lee is one of the top rebounders in the NBA. He is also becoming a much better scorer. Young forward Wilson Chandler can score and rebound well, too. Nate Robinson is one of the best jumpers in the NBA. He won the 2009 **Slam Dunk** Contest!

25

Nate Robinson is one of the best leapers in the NBA.

Gearing Up

New York Knicks players wear a uniform and special basketball sneakers. Some wear other pads to protect themselves. Check out this picture of Wilson Chandler and learn about what NBA players wear.

The Basketball

NBA basketballs are made of leather. Several pieces are held together with rubber edges. Inside the leather ball is a hollow ball of rubber. This is filled with air. The leather is covered with little bumps called "pebbles." The pebbles help players get a good grip on the ball. The basketball used in the Women's National Basketball Association (WNBA) is slightly smaller than the men's basketball.

Jersey

Shorts

Socks

Basketball shoes

Wilson Chandler battles against a tough defender.

Sports Stats

Note: All numbers shown are through the 2008–2009 season.

HIGH SCORERS

These players have scored the most points for the Knicks.

PLAYER	POINTS
Patrick Ewing	23,665
Walt Frazier	14,617

HELPING HAND

Here are the Knicks' all-time leaders in **assists**.

PLAYER	ASSISTS
Walt Frazier	4,791
Mark Jackson	4,005

CLEANING THE BOARDS

Rebounds are a big part of the game.
Here are the Knicks' best rebounders.

PLAYER	REBOUNDS
Patrick Ewing	10,759
Willis Reed	8,414

MOST THREE-POINT SHOTS MADE

Shots taken from behind a line about 23 feet (7 m) from the basket are worth three points. Here are the Knicks' best at these long-distance shots.

PLAYER	THREE-POINT SHOTS
John Starks	982
Allan Houston	921

COACH

Who coached the Knicks to the most wins?

Red Holzman, 613

Glossary

assists passes to teammates that lead directly to making baskets

center a player (usually the tallest on the team) who plays close to the basket

defense when a team doesn't have the ball and is trying to keep the other team from scoring

forward one of two tall players who rebound and score near the basket

guard one of two players who set up plays, pass to teammates closer to the basket, and shoot from farther away

NBA Finals the seven-game NBA championship series, in which the champion must win four games

offense when a team has the ball and is trying to score

playoffs a series of games between 16 teams that decide which two teams will play in the NBA Finals

rebounds missed shots that bounce off the backboard or rim and are often grabbed by another player

rivalry an ongoing competition between teams that play each other often, over a long time

slam dunk a shot in which a player stuffs the ball into the basket

tournaments series of games where a large number of teams compete to see who is the winner

Find Out More

Books

Christopher, Matt. *Greatest Moments in Basketball History.* New York: Little, Brown, 2009.

Craats, Rennay. *Basketball.* Toronto: Weigl Publishers, 2008.

Hareas, John. *Eyewitness Basketball.* New York: DK, 2005.

Stewart, Mark. *The New York Knicks.* Chicago: Norwood House Press, 2006.

Web Sites

Visit our Web page for links about the New York Knicks and other NBA teams:

childsworld.com/links

Note to Parents, Teachers, and Librarians: We routinely verify our Web links to make sure they are safe, active sites—so encourage your readers to check them out!

Index

K. C. KELLEY

K. C. Kelley has written dozens of books on basketball, football, baseball, and other sports for young readers. K. C. used to work for NFL Publishing and has covered several Super Bowls. He likes to watch any basketball game, but the Los Angeles Lakers are his favorite team.